NATIVE * AMERICAN * CULTURE

THE EUROPEAN INVASION

Barbara McCall

Series Editor
Jordan E. Kerber, Ph.D.

* * *

ROURKE PUBLICATIONS, INC.
Vero Beach, Florida 32964

Printed in the United States of America.

A Blackbirch Graphics book.

Library of Congress Cataloging-in-Publication Data

McCall, Barbara, A., 1936–
The European Invasion / by Barbara McCall.
    p.   cm. — (Native American culture)
    Includes bibliographical references and index.
    ISBN 0-86625-535-4
    1. Indians—First contact with Europeans—Juvenile literature. 2. America—Discovery and exploration—Juvenile literature. 3. Europe—Colonies—America—Juvenile literature. [1. Indians—First contact with Europeans. 2. America—Discovey and exploration.] I. Title. II. Series.
E59.F53M33   1994
970.01—dc20   94-5530
                                                                          CIP
                                                                          AC

Contents

Introduction

The words "Native American" and "Indian" create strong images for many people. Some may think of fierce warriors with bows and arrows, tomahawks, and rifles who battled the U.S. Cavalry in the days of the Wild West. Others probably imagine a proud and peaceful people who just hunted buffalo and lived in tipis on the Great Plains. These are just some of the popular stereotypes of Native Americans, and like most stereotypes they give a false impression.

This series on *Native American Culture* presents six books on various aspects of Native American life: tribal law, childrearing, arts and crafts, daily life, spiritual life, and the invasion by Europe. By reading these books, you will learn that there is no single Native American culture, but instead many different ones. Each Native American group or tribe in the past, as well as today, is a separate nation. While tribes may share some similarities, many are as different from one another as the English are from the Spanish.

The geographic focus of this series is the North American continent (United States and Canada), with special attention to the area within the present-day United States. However, Native Americans have lived, and continue to live, in Central America and South America. In addition, the authors of each book draw upon a wealth of historical information mainly from a time between the 1500s and 1900s, when most Native Americans were first contacted by European explorers, conquerors, and settlers. Much is known about this period of Native American life from documents and observations recorded by Europeans who came to North America.

It is also important to understand that Native Americans have a much longer and more complex history on the continent than just the past 500 years. Archaeologists have excavated ancient Native American sites as old as 12,000 years. The people who lived at these sites were among the first residents of North America. They did not keep written records of their lives, so the only information known about them comes from their stone tools and other remains that they left behind. We do know that during the thousands of years of Native American settlement across the continent the cultures of these early inhabitants changed in many important ways. Some of these cultures disappeared a long time ago, while others have survived and continue to change today. Indeed, there are more than 1.5 million Native Americans currently living in the United States, and the federal government recognizes over 500 tribes. Native Americans are in all walks of life, and many still practice traditions and speak the languages of their ancestors. About 250,000 Native Americans presently live on some 278 reservations in the country.

The books in this series capture the wonderful richness and variety of Native American life from different time periods. They remind us that the story of America begins with Native Americans. They also provide more accurate images of Native Americans, images that I hope will enable you to challenge the stereotypes.

Jordan E. Kerber, Ph.D.
Director of Native American Studies
Colgate University

Chapter

1

The Early Visitors

Opposite:
On his famous journeys to the "New World," Christopher Columbus called the people whom he met "Indians" because he believed he had arrived in India. European explorers such as Columbus did not acknowledge that the land they "discovered" actually belonged to native peoples who had already been there for thousands of years.

About 500 years before Columbus landed in the Americas, the Vikings settled portions of Greenland. Norseman Erik Thorvaldsson (known as "Erik the Red") sailed from Iceland around A.D. 982 and landed in Greenland around A.D. 985. In the 990s, Leif Eriksson, son of Erik, landed in Greenland and possibly Labrador, Newfoundland, and New Brunswick. The Norse settled along the eastern coast of Labrador between A.D. 1000 and 1300.

Archaeological materials belonging to the Norse have been excavated at Norse and Inuit (Eskimo) sites in the northeastern Arctic. Some Norse goods have been found at Native American archaeological sites as far south as Maine, but they were obtained through trade with Inuit groups to the north after the Norse abandoned their settlements. By the 1100s or before, the Norse had direct contact with local Inuits and likely contact with Beothuks, Algonquian-speaking Native Americans who visited Labrador and

Newfoundland during summers. Unlike the later European expeditions to the Americas, the Norse voyages to the northeastern Arctic were not made to colonize or convert the native populations. Rather, the Norse were in search of firewood for their homeland in Iceland.

Europeans came to the Americas for many reasons. The first groups were adventurers, like Christopher Columbus, who came to explore the New World. After exploring a part of the land, the Europeans claimed the territory for their own countries. They did not recognize that the land already belonged to those who lived here—the Native Americans.

In the 1500s, Spanish conquistadors invaded the area in the United States that is now the Southeast (specifically, Florida, Tennessee, Georgia, Alabama, and South Carolina), parts of the Southwest (Arizona and New Mexico), Mexico, South America, and several small islands in the Caribbean. *Conquistador* is the Spanish word for "conqueror." These soldiers came wearing heavy suits of armor and traveled on horseback looking for gold, silver, and other riches. They brought their horses with them, and this was the first time the horse was seen on the continent since a slightly different species had become extinct at the end of the Ice Age.

The Spanish conquistadors encountered the Native Americans who lived in these areas, and treated them like slaves. Along with the Christian missionaries who accompanied them, the conquistadors forced the Native Americans to accept Spanish ways. These priests built missions—outposts with a church, school, and other buildings—where they tried to convert the Native Americans to Christianity. Only a few tribes successfully resisted the foreigners.

The invaders from Spain, and those who followed from other European countries, also brought diseases with them that killed whole villages of native people. Until the Europeans arrived, the Native Americans had never had measles,

＊

9

This Navajo cave painting depicts the arrival of a Spanish priest along with conquistadors on horseback. When the Spanish arrived in the North American Southwest, they used military might to force Native Americans to follow European ways.

typhus, smallpox, or cholera, and had built up no resistance to them. They suffered terribly during large outbreaks of these diseases, called epidemics.

By the early 1600s, the French began invading the lands of the Native Americans in the North. The French sailed the St. Lawrence and Mississippi rivers and traveled the forest pathways around the Great Lakes and in the Ohio Valley to fully explore these regions.

Like the Spanish, the French were looking for riches. The French were primarily interested in beaver fur. They conducted a very profitable fur trade with the Native Americans. In exchange for furs, the native peoples received goods they had never seen before. They acquired metal pots, steel needles, woven blankets, cloth of many colors,

This Currier and Ives engraving shows a group of fur trappers sitting around a campfire with Native Americans of the northwestern region. In many cases, the first Europeans that Native Americans actually encountered were trappers, hunters, and traders.

and other useful European goods. Unfortunately, they were also introduced to liquor and firearms.

The French did not enslave the Native Americans as the Spanish did. They also did not establish new towns and villages for their families as the English were doing, many miles to the south. The French, however, lured the native peoples into trapping and trading more fur skins by giving them firearms and liquor. Many Frenchmen came as traders, trappers, and hunters. They often lived in the deep forests

or in nearby forts that had been built by the French soldiers. Missionaries from France also came to convert the native people to Christianity. Unlike the Spanish, however, French priests did not set up large missions. Instead, they lived among the Native Americans who would accept them.

The abundance of fur in the New World also attracted the English and the Dutch. The race to bring in more and thus acquire European goods made the Native American tribes rivals, just as the French, Dutch, and English were already rivals. The Mohawk tribe, for example, slaughtered thousands of their rival Native Americans in an attempt to control the fur trade. Later, during the French and Indian War, the Mohawk sided with the English while other tribes sided with the French in the struggle to gain control of territory in North America.

In the 1600s, while the French were gathering furs for sale in Europe, groups of English people sailed for North America. They were neither conquerors nor traders. They were settlers. They viewed the New World on the Atlantic Coast as their new homeland. They set up colonies in present-day Virginia, Massachusetts, Rhode Island, Pennsylvania, and other places.

The Native Americans who were living in each area accepted the strangers in different ways. Some groups showed curiosity and friendliness. Others were hostile. It depended on how the strangers acted during the first days of contact.

In some places, like Rhode Island and Pennsylvania, the natives and the foreigners lived together peacefully for several years. Each group learned from the other. The natives helped the settlers survive in an unfamiliar land. The foreigners made a great effort to treat the Native Americans fairly and with respect.

In a short time, however, more and more English settlers built towns along the rivers and valleys of the East Coast. The settlers invaded the open spaces where the native peoples once hunted, gathered, and farmed. The foreigners and their families intended to own the land where they settled. The idea of owning land had been unknown to Native Americans. They believed land belonged to a whole tribe that had lived in a certain place for centuries.

Gradually, the Native Americans were drawn into the rivalry between the French and English over control of part of North America. The French and English set up military forts along the St. Lawrence River and in the Ohio Valley. The English had forts along the seacoast, as well.

The French and English made friends with many tribes in order to get their support in the new lands. The English had allies among the Iroquois and others. The French developed loyal followers among the Huron. The Ottawa people, led by the great chief Pontiac, were strong military supporters of the French during the French and Indian War.

By the time the Revolutionary War ended in 1783, many Native Americans of the Northeast had been pushed off their lands or killed. Some went to Canada. Others moved west of the Mississippi River. By that time, the Native Americans of the Great Plains and the Pacific Northwest were just beginning to experience the invasion of their homelands by white people.

The settlers transformed the colonies into the new country of the United States. Once free-roaming, Native Americans were slowly forced to live on reservations, lands that were set aside for tribes but were controlled by the U.S. and Canadian governments. Living on a reservation meant a loss of freedom to hunt, gather, or fish outside the reservation boundaries. It also meant a loss of much of the old cultures and traditions.

Not all Native Americans were resettled on reservations. Some Iroquois went to Canada. Other groups managed to survive apart from tribal life. They married among the "invaders" and their descendants.

Over the years, many Native Americans slowly adopted the ways of the white people. Each new generation of Native Americans lost more of the old ways. Yet many managed to keep some of their traditions alive. Today, Native Americans are striving to re-establish their languages, traditions, and sense of cultural identity.

Chapter

2

The Spanish Influence

Beginning with Juan Ponce de León, in 1513, many Spanish explorers passed through present-day Florida, Texas, and other areas along the coast of the Gulf of Mexico. In 1539, Hernando de Soto and his Spanish soldiers first entered Florida and traveled the lands north and west. At first, the Native Americans greeted him with gifts and food. They soon learned, however, that the stranger and his men did not want to be friends. The strangers were invaders who wanted slaves to do their work.

The Native Americans of the Southeast were not easily conquered. They fought the invaders fiercely and burned the missions run by Franciscan priests. One mission, St. Augustine, established in 1565, did succeed.

Over time, many Native Americans moved closer to this Spanish mission. By the late 1600s, the mission of St. Augustine was viewed by the Native Americans as a place for protection against the British, who were invading from the north. Today, St. Augustine is the oldest city in the United States.

Opposite:
A major objective for most Europeans who settled in the New World was the conversion of the native peoples to Christianity. Missions founded by Spanish priests were among the first non-Native American buildings constructed in North America, and were intended to "civilize" the non-believers.

Soldiers and Firearms

When de Soto reached a Creek village in what is now the state of Alabama, he demanded that the chief there call together the leaders of nearby villages to welcome the Spanish soldiers. Chief Tuscalusa, however, was ready for him.

Tuscalusa warned the others of trouble. When de Soto and his men rode into the village of Mabila, now called Mobile, the Creek men were waiting with weapons. A battle followed. The bows and arrows of the Creek, however, were no match for the guns of the Spanish. More than 2,500 Creek died in the struggle, but the Spanish were finally driven away.

Farther west, in 1540, Francisco de Coronado led his Spanish army into present-day Arizona and New Mexico in

This drawing, by famous American artist Frederic Remington, depicts Francisco de Coronado in 1540. In his search for gold, Coronado encountered Native American tribes and, in some cases, did battle with them.

search of the Seven Cities of Cibola—the "seven cities of gold." He had heard from the natives of New Spain, now called Mexico, that the cities in the North held great storehouses of this precious metal. Even the streets were said to be paved with gold.

Coronado, however, found no gold. Instead, he and his 230 horse soldiers and 62 foot soldiers came upon villages of stone and clay. First, they encountered the village of the Zuni people, then the Hopi. The villagers had been warned of Coronado's coming and greeted the invaders with a storm of arrows.

Their arrows fell against suits of armor, causing little harm to the Spanish. The Spanish were equipped with muskets and horses. Many Zuni and Hopi men died in the encounter. Native Americans had never seen firearms or these strange animals. Both were frightening, but guns and horses would one day become important in the lives of Native Americans of the West.

News of Coronado's army spread quickly. As he rode throughout the Southwest, other tribes greeted him with gifts rather than arrows. The soldiers ate the corn stored in the villages and continued their search. Disappointed in their quest for riches, the Spanish forces returned to Mexico.

Coronado called the stone and clay village of the natives a pueblo, the Spanish word for "town." The tribes that lived in pueblos came to be known as the Pueblo people. The lands that Coronado ranged are now called the Four Corners, where New Mexico, Arizona, Utah, and Colorado meet.

Spanish Missions

Between 1580 and 1598, other Spanish soldiers returned to the area of the Pueblo people and took control of their villages. The Spanish needed slaves to grow their crops and do other work. They brought Catholic priests with them

The ruins of the Pecos Mission still stand in Pecos Pueblo, New Mexico. The Spanish who ran such missions enslaved Native Americans of the Southwest and forced them to abandon their customs and beliefs in favor of Christianity and European ways.

who set up missions. These priests introduced the Pueblo tribes to the Christian religion and European ways.

Over time, Spanish priests forced Native Americans to give up their own religious and tribal customs. The Pueblo people were forbidden to worship the Great Spirit in ways they had done for centuries. They continued, however, to conduct ceremonies and other traditional activities in secret. When the Spanish found their rules were not being obeyed, they reacted with brutality. The native people were often beaten. They were even burned at the stake for refusing to accept Spanish customs.

Spanish missions included schools. Priests trained Native Americans to speak and write Spanish. They taught them to become carpenters and builders. They set up farms and ranches with cattle, horses, sheep, and goats. All of these foreign ways were forced upon Native Americans.

They were no substitute for the freedom to live in their traditional ways.

Native Americans of the pueblos were dominated by the Spanish for years. In 1660, the Southwest experienced the start of a severe drought. Years passed with little rain. Crops failed, and famine spread throughout the area. What food could be found went to the Spanish. The Native Americans grew increasingly bitter.

From time to time, the people of the pueblos attempted to rebel against the oppression of the Spanish. Each time an uprising was uncovered, the people were punished severely.

The Pueblo Revolt

By 1680, a strong leader named Popé was able to organize the people of the pueblos. Popé had once been severely whipped by the Spanish for refusing to accept Christianity. He hated the Spanish and plotted rebellion.

From a pueblo in Taos, Popé sent runners to all villages for hundreds of miles. Each runner carried a knotted rope. The knots marked the number of days left before the revolt, which was planned for August 13. Unfortunately, the Spanish captured one of the runners and learned of the plot against them.

The Native Americans swiftly changed their plans and moved up the day of the attack. On August 11, at Taos, New Mexico, they surprised the Spanish, who were unprepared. Within a few days, more than 400 Spanish were dead and Spanish churches and ranches were in flames.

On August 14, Popé and his followers laid siege to Santa Fe, New Mexico, the Spanish capital in the region. The battle raged for more than a week. When it was over, all the Spanish had been driven out of the area. They were forced to retreat to El Paso, Texas, several hundred miles to the south. The Pueblo Revolt is considered the most spectacular and successful rebellion of Native Americans against Europeans anywhere in North America.

Popé controlled the area until he died in 1692. Then the Spanish regained control of the pueblo villages and once again tried to establish missions. They had some success, except among the Hopi people. The Hopi resisted all interference by Europeans. As soon as missions were built, the Hopi men burned them down, killing everyone present. The Spanish never bothered the Hopi again.

The Arrival of the Horse

The Spanish invasion of the Southwest destroyed the ancient ways of life for many Native Americans. However, the invaders introduced the horse to North America. The horse was a valuable addition to the lives of the people living on the Great Plains and in the Northwest.

The Spanish brought with them many Arabian and Andalusian horses. When the native peoples first saw the large animal they did not know what to call it. Some called it a "big dog," while others named it an "elk dog" because of its size. Over time, native peoples captured runaway horses. They also tamed wild mustangs they found in the canyons and deserts.

By the late 1600s, some tribes of the West had developed new breeds of horses. One tribe became excellent horse breeders. They were the Nez Perce, who lived in the deep valleys of the Bitterroot Mountains in present-day Idaho and Montana. The Nez Perce developed the spotted-rumped Appaloosa, which became a prized possession first of Native Americans and, later, of white people.

The horse greatly influenced the daily lives of the Native Americans of the Great Plains—the Sioux, Cheyenne, Crow, Arapaho, and Comanche, to name a few. These tribes were once farmers, buffalo hunters, and wild plant gatherers. As

This illustration by famous American artist George Caitlin shows a Crow and his horse adorned in ceremonial costume. The introduction of horses to North America by the Spanish changed the lives of Native Americans in many significant ways.

they obtained more horses, they gradually stopped farming. By the late 1700s and early 1800s, these tribes spent most of their time following buffalo herds, for they depended on the buffalo for food, clothing, and shelter.

The horse made it possible for the tribes of the Northwest and the Rocky Mountains to travel farther and more easily. The Walla Walla, Cayuse, and Nez Perce tribes traveled from present-day eastern Washington, Oregon, and Idaho south into California. People learned more about their distant neighbors. They traded more goods and learned new skills. Beginning in the mid-1800s, the horse aided Native Americans in their battles against the U.S. Cavalry.

California Missions

In 1769, Father Junipero Serra, a Spanish priest, founded the mission of San Diego de Alcala. It was the first of twenty-one missions built in California. From San Diego to San Francisco, Spanish priests and soldiers ran the missions. A California mission had hundreds of acres of land with a church, a school, farms, cattle, small huts for the Native Americans, and large quarters for the Spanish.

The mission was the instrument the Spanish used to "civilize" the native peoples of the area. Also, a mission was used to prevent a takeover of Spanish-owned territory by other Europeans. The Spanish, and most other Europeans, believed the natives were savages.

During the next sixty-five years, much of the Native American cultures along the coast of California were slowly destroyed. Spanish missionaries and soldiers succeeded in turning these peoples into converts or slaves. Native Americans who did not accept Christianity and European ways were beaten or shackled in irons until they converted.

Missionaries often traveled deep into the North American wilderness to seek out native peoples that they could convert to Christianity.

The Lusieño tribe of about 3,000 people accepted mission life. They became farmers and cattle ranchers. They learned the Spanish language and European ways. They also experienced epidemics of European diseases that many did not survive. Great numbers of Lusieños died.

By 1821, the California missions came to an end. The Mexican government took over the land from Spain for a short time. In 1848, the United States acquired California from Mexico. Some Native Americans were moved to reservations. Others attempted to survive among the new Americans.

Chapter

3

French Traders

By the early 1500s, fishermen from Portugal, France, and England were making yearly trips across the Atlantic. Their destination was the Grand Banks off the coast of Newfoundland, Canada. There they fished for cod and other varieties of fish that they took back to Europe.

The fishermen made brief contacts with the Native Americans from time to time. At that point, all they wanted was fish. In 1524, the culture of the Native Americans of the Northeast changed. In that year, Jacques Cartier, a French explorer, traveled the St. Lawrence River and the lands along its banks. He claimed the lands as a French territory and called it New France.

Cartier had seen the native peoples trading beaver skins with the fishermen in return for their strong nets and metal hooks. Aware of the value of beaver fur in European markets, he knew he had discovered a source of great wealth.

A few Frenchmen came to the area in the following years in search of fur. By 1608, Samuel de Champlain led

Opposite:
Because many
European settlers
in the North and
Northwest were French
trappers and hunters,
there was much French
influence on the
Native American
tribes of those regions.
Here, a Native
American trapper
wears a French
trapper's hat and
carries a gun of
European origin.

the first French invasion. He brought soldiers and traders to North America to control the fur trade. He established a fortified trading post in what is now the city of Quebec, Canada.

Many who were not soldiers came only to trap and live in the wilderness. They wandered on their own and lived in huts and wigwams, like the Algonquian and Iroquoian speaking peoples of the area. These early Frenchmen were called "vagabonds of the forest"—people who moved from place to place. They lived peacefully among the Native Americans and attempted to be friends.

Knives, Axes, and Muskets

The Huron, Iroquois, and other tribes of the Northeast were eager to trade their furs and corn for the things the Frenchmen brought—metal knives and axes, steel needles, copper pots, blankets, and more.

The native peoples had never seen such luxuries. They enjoyed the European goods. With sharp metal axes, they could more easily cut trees for building canoes. With woven blankets and European cloth, they did not have to hunt animals and then process their skins for clothing. Even metal was flattened and cut into tips for arrows.

The more European goods the natives acquired, the more they wanted. European goods reduced the dependence of Native Americans on their environment. These goods also made Native Americans increasingly dependent on Europeans.

Over time, the great demand for fur changed the way these tribes lived. Before the invasion of the white people, Native Americans killed animals because they needed food and clothing. Hunters were careful to leave enough of each breed for the next year. Unfortunately, that environmental concern ended with the coming of European greed.

Native Americans who once farmed gave up farming. Those who had hunted deer and moose spent more time trapping beaver and other small animals, whose furs were in demand. Beaver, once plentiful, became scarce. As the supply of fur decreased, rivalry among tribes increased.

Champlain and the French were eager to turn Native Americans into allies—friends who would fight with them against common enemies. The French knew they would need the Native Americans as allies because other Europeans wanted a share in the wealth of the fur trade.

The first people Champlain met were the Iroquoian-speaking Huron. He joined them in a battle near the lake that is now named for him. The Huron were fighting their neighbors, the Mohawk. Supplied with European muskets, the Huron warriors easily overpowered the Mohawk. More than one hundred Mohawk men were killed by the Frenchmen and their fire-spitting muskets.

After this battle, the Mohawk tribe harbored a hostility toward the French. It was the start of a rivalry that would not end until after the French and Indian War, more than 150 years later. The Mohawk, nonetheless, were willing to trade with the French when the tribe could benefit. The Mohawk became one of the most powerful tribes of the Northeast. They were also one of the five tribes making up the Iroquois Confederacy, or Iroquois League. In time, the Iroquois gained control over much of the lands in the East.

The Huron as Middlemen

The French made allies with the Huron tribe that lived between the Great Lakes and the St. Lawrence River. French missionaries converted the Huron to Christianity. In 1615, the French and the Huron signed a trade alliance that lasted until 1629. The Huron agreed to supply the French with up to 12,000 beaver and otter skins each year.

✳

28

The Huron did not trap all the animals themselves. They were clever businesspeople. They traded their corn and European goods with other tribes that lived west or north of the Great Lakes. There, the small animals were more plentiful. From these tribes, the Huron obtained furs. Acting as middlemen, the Huron then turned around and sold the furs to the French.

As middlemen, the Huron had two main suppliers—the Nipissings, who trapped as far north as Hudson Bay, and the Ottawa, who collected furs from many tribes to the west. The Ottawa were also good middlemen. The name Ottawa means "to trade." Like the Huron, they did not catch many beaver, but they bartered, or traded, for fur in exchange for whatever another tribe might need. They traveled the lakes and rivers in their well-made birchbark canoes, which were loaded with corn, sunflower oil, rugs, tobacco, medicinal herbs, and roots.

Individual Ottawa families controlled the trade routes around the Great Lakes. They gave or denied permission to others to use the waterways. Those who used the routes illegally had to pay a fine in the form of food or fur. Some trespassers were even killed.

The trade for European goods made certain tribes very powerful. Before the arrival of white traders with guns, the tribes, if they fought at all, fought mainly over territory to which they claimed hunting and fishing rights. After the arrival of Europeans, however, the Native Americans fought with one another more frequently, as they became increasingly eager to have European goods. Eventually, many Native Americans fought against the white men to get back land that they and their ancestors had lived on for thousands of years.

Tribes from the interior of the country often felt cheated because the tribes acting as middlemen kept the

The Ottawa were successful fur traders in the 1600s. They traveled the waters of the North in birchbark canoes, like the one being built in this engraving. They collected furs from other tribes in exchange for valuable goods.

better European goods for themselves. Tribal quarrels became common. Skirmishes led to larger conflicts. Groups often fought with each other because one group got a better deal.

The need to find more and more beaver fur for trade fueled the hostilities of the warlike Mohawk. They began stealing boatloads of furs from their neighbors to trade with the Europeans. Eventually, the Mohawk destroyed many of their neighbors in a series of battles called the Beaver Wars.

Competition from the Dutch

In the early 1600s, about the same time the Huron were making contact with Champlain, the Mohegan were welcoming Henry Hudson, an English navigator hired by the Dutch. Hudson arrived in the Mohegan village of Schotak, a few hundred miles to the south of the Huron settlement, near the present city of Albany, New York.

The Mohegan chief welcomed Hudson with food, and they dined in the chief's longhouse, the dwelling typical of Iroquois and nearby tribes. Hudson brought goods to

trade—knives and hatchets and other metal goods, just like the French. He also brought small, shiny glass beads that had great appeal to the people in the village.

The colorful Dutch beads looked like the wampum beads that inland tribes were accustomed to trading with tribes that lived along the coast. The coastal tribes worked very hard to make wampum beads from seashells. White wampum beads were made from the inside of a conch or whelk—a large saltwater snail. Purple wampum beads were made from the quahog—a saltwater clam. In time, the Dutch and other European countries developed tools to easily manufacture wampum, which they traded for furs.

The Mohegan signed a treaty with the Dutch in 1613, letting them build a trading post along the river that was later named for Hudson. The Mohegan also controlled the access of other tribes to the Dutch. They demanded a gift from each tribe that brought furs to the foreigners. Other tribes did not like this control and fought back.

The Mohawk resented being cut out of the Dutch trade. They fought to change the balance of power. Joined by other tribes from the North, they attacked the Mohegan and took over control of the Dutch fur trade about 1624.

The Mohegan were forced to relocate on the east side of the Hudson River. In time, the Mohawk and Mohegan settled their disputes. Together, they controlled the wampum trade, which was made more profitable once the Dutch introduced tools to make the beads more quickly. They used wampum to weave belts that recorded treaties and other major events of their lives. Today, the Iroquois still preserve many of these historic wampum belts.

Iroquois Control

The Iroquoian speaking tribes—the Mohawk, Seneca, Onondaga, Oneida, and Cayuga—had formed an alliance, or confederacy. They agreed to live in peace and harmony with one another. After the arrival of Europeans, the Iroquois Confederacy became the powerhouse in the East. From 1649 to 1650, the Iroquois, armed with European muskets, massacred more than 10,000 neighbors, including the Huron, who were loyal to the French.

After 1650, the Iroquois Confederacy ruled the territory from the St. Lawrence River to Georgia and from New England to Michigan. The Iroquois took over the fur trade with both the French and the Dutch. They collected gifts from tribes that wanted to exchange beaver fur for tools.

By 1664, the Dutch had been forced out of the area by the English, who were also driving Native Americans off their lands along the East Coast.

During historic times, the Iroquois Confederacy controlled much of what is now the northeastern United States and southeastern Canada. The center of their homeland was, and still is, within the present-day state of New York.

Chapter

4

English and Dutch Settlers

The English came to North America to make permanent homes. Unlike the French, they were settlers who planned to stay and raise families. The New World offered them plenty of wide-open space, a chance for profit, and a way to escape the rules of harsh kings and queens.

The Native Americans allowed the first groups of English settlers to live among them peacefully. They even signed treaties and "sold" land to the strangers. These first Native Americans who sold land, however, did not understand the idea of owning or selling land. In the early years, when a chief put his mark on a piece of paper, he did not realize how that mark would affect the future. Often he did not understand that his tribe thereby gave up its rights to live on the land where its ancestors had lived for thousands of years. Most likely, the chief thought he was agreeing to let the strangers use the land for a period of time.

Native Americans and settlers had different views of life. Native Americans believed the land and its riches were the

Opposite:
The great chief Powhatan was the leader of the Tidewater Confederacy, which was a coalition of tribes along the Chesapeake Bay. Without the help of Chief Powhatan and his people, the first English settlement at Jamestown would never have taken place.

gift of the Great Spirit and should be treated with great respect and they used its resources with this in mind. The settlers wanted to own and alter the land. As farmers, they cut down the forests and drove away the small animals that supplied the Native Americans with food and clothing.

With these differences, conflicts were unavoidable. A steady stream of new settlers forced the Native Americans to give up their lands, their means of supporting themselves, and their freedom. Sometimes the Native Americans began an attack. Other times the settlers started the skirmish. An attack was always followed by a counterattack. Sometimes the retaliation came a year or more later. Revenge was often a strong motive for war, just as it is among countries today.

In the 1500s, when the first European invasion began, there were more than 1 million Native Americans living here. By the end of the 1800s, their population had been reduced to about 200,000 people.

In Virginia

In 1607, Captain John Smith and 144 English colonists reached the coast of Virginia. Chief Powhatan was the powerful leader of the Tidewater Confederacy, also called the Powhatan Confederacy, of tribes along the Chesapeake Bay. Chief Powhatan's native name was Wahunsonacock, but he was called Powhatan by John Smith and his group after the location of the chief's residence at Powhatan on the James River falls, the site of present-day of Richmond, Virginia.

At first, Powhatan was angry with John Smith's party because they broke into his storehouse and stole corn. Powhatan's young daughter, Pocahontas, pleaded with her father to spare Smith's life and the lives of his party. A legend says that Pocahontas threw her head into Smith's lap as her father was about to strike Smith with a stone club.

According to legend, Chief Powhatan's daughter, Pocahontas (right), saved Captain John Smith's life by pleading with her father to spare the Englishman.

Without Powhatan's help, the colonists would not have succeeded in Jamestown, the name they gave to their new colony. He taught the English how to cultivate crops of corn. He led them to the best places to fish. He also showed them how to use tree bark to build their huts.

Pocahontas was about twelve when she met John Smith and the English. She helped to keep a friendly feeling among the strangers and her people. Still, it was an uneasy peace. Pocahontas later married one of the colonists, John Rolfe, whom she met while she was held hostage by the English after John Smith left for England in 1609. Their marriage in 1614 extended the peace for a few more years. When Pocahontas visited London with her husband, she was celebrated as the "Indian Princess." Shortly afterward she fell ill and died.

Powhatan's successor, Chief Opechancanough, no longer accepted the English. More colonists continued to crowd the natives. In 1622, he organized the first coordinated attack on the colonists. More than 300 English settlers were killed.

The English never forgave those who murdered their friends and families. They burned the cornfields of more than 1,100 natives. It was a punishment to remind them of the growing power of the English.

Once again, in 1644, the natives tried to drive the invaders off their lands. This time, the English assembled several thousand colonists. It was a decisive victory for the English. They forced the tribes living along the York, James, and Blackwater rivers to give up their lands. In return, the English agreed not to move further inland. However, they did not honor their agreement.

By 1677, the tribes of the Chesapeake Bay were forced onto a reservation, away from the coast. They had to give up their rights to all remaining territory. The English also demanded a yearly payment in the form of food or fur.

In New Netherlands

While the English were taking control of the Chesapeake Bay area, the Dutch were moving into the adjoining territory to the north. The Dutch came first as fur traders from the Dutch West India Company. Only a small number of Dutch invaded the lands of Native Americans. They traded along the Hudson River and Long Island Sound.

The fur business gradually became unprofitable. The Dutch then traded their goods for land and, like the English, became farmers. In 1626, the Dutch "bought" an island from Chief Manhasset of the Manhattan tribe. The value of the trade was later calculated to be about twenty-four dollars worth of Dutch goods.

That agreement was the second one that the Dutch had negotiated for the same island. Their first deal was with men of the Canarsee tribe. Shortly after, the Manhattan tribe demanded goods from the Dutch because they said the land had never belonged to the Canarsee tribe. The Dutch named the island New Amsterdam, and they called all their possessions New Netherlands.

By 1639, New Amsterdam was a very busy city filled with merchants—men who brought all kinds of goods from Europe and traded them out of shops in the city. They also set up farms, but farming was less successful. Nevertheless, the presence of the Dutch in New Amsterdam caused conflicts with the Native Americans of the area.

The Dutch, with the help of their Mohawk friends, attacked the Wappinger tribe. This attack was called the Slaughter of the Innocents because so many men, women, and children were killed while they slept in their wigwams.

The Wappingers and other area tribes joined together to retaliate against the Dutch. From 1643 to 1644, the Native Americans held the area in siege. The English built a wall around New Amsterdam for protection. Today, New York City's Wall Street marks the location of the wall. Eventually, the English came to the aid of the Dutch and defeated the natives. Twenty years later, the English pushed the Dutch out of New Amsterdam and changed the name to New York.

Before the Dutch left the area, they caused more trouble and great pain for the Native Americans. About 1660, Peter Stuyvesant, the governor of New Netherlands, ordered his people to take Native American children as hostages. This order was part of a plan to force the tribal leaders to submit to Dutch demands. Some Native Americans submitted right away. Others did not. Tragically, many Native American children lived for several years in terror among strangers.

In Massachusetts

The English reached Plymouth, Massachusetts, a few years before the Dutch moved into New Amsterdam. The survival of these Pilgrim settlers depended on the generosity of Native Americans, who chose to help the strangers.

Months after the Pilgrims arrived in 1620, they made contact with two young men who spoke English. One was Samoset, a Pemaquid sachem, or chief, who met the Pilgrims when they landed on Cape Cod in 1620 (prior to the Plymouth landing). The other was Squanto, whose real name was Tisquantum. He had been kidnapped several years earlier and taken to Europe as a slave by an English sea captain. Tisquantum finally escaped and made his way back to his homeland.

Samoset greets a Pilgrim family in Massachusetts. Many Native Americans offered help and advice to the Pilgrims.

Tisquantum taught the English all they needed to know to survive in a strange, harsh land. Like Powhatan's tribe in Jamestown, the natives in Plymouth showed the white people how to grow corn, squash, and beans. Tisquantum also introduced the Pilgrims to Chief Massasoit of the Wampanoag tribe. Although the Pilgrims were invaders of the Wampanoag lands, they were peaceful people and the Native Americans treated them well. Some scientists have estimated that up to 95 percent of the Wampanoag tribe in the vicinity of Plymouth died between 1616 and 1619 due to European diseases that were spread by European traders and fishermen.

After their first harvest in Plymouth, the Pilgrims invited their Wampanoag neighbors to celebrate a feast and to give thanks. We now commemorate that event each November as a national holiday—Thanksgiving.

By 1621, Chief Massasoit and the Pilgrims, led by John Carver, signed a treaty to live together peacefully. It was the first such agreement between Native Americans and colonists.

Chief Massasoit always treated the English with kindness and friendship. He even sided with them when other tribes attacked the settlers. The harmony, however, ended after his death. The Wampanoag people were treated very badly by the new settlers, who came in increasing numbers.

It became a policy of the Plymouth Colony to punish Native Americans who broke the rules of the colony. A Wampanoag man or woman was often dragged before an English judge and sentenced to the same penalty as a white person for breaking the law. The penalty might be a day in the stocks, a beating, or much worse. The cutting off of a person's ear or a finger for improper behavior on the Sabbath—the Lord's day—was not uncommon.

The two sons of Chief Massasoit—Wamsutta and Metacomet—became the new leaders of the tribe. They grew to hate the English for the way the Native Americans were being humiliated and for the way the English were taking land away from them. It is suspected that Wamsutta was poisoned by the English. For several years, Metacomet made plans to drive the invaders off his lands. He secretly sent runners to neighboring tribes to persuade them to join his people in an alliance against the English.

Before the alliance was firmly established, a series of fierce attacks began. By 1675, fighting broke out in many places across New England. Sometimes the native people started the fight, and other times the white people were responsible. The colonial militia—usually just a group of farmers with muskets—burned villages and fields of nearby Native American tribes.

Metacomet, called King Philip by the English, was finally captured in the battle of the Great Swamp, near Kingston, Rhode Island. He escaped only to be caught again and killed in 1676 in present-day Bristol, Rhode Island. The English captured many natives, including Metacomet's wife and son, and sold them as slaves to traders going to the Caribbean Islands.

More than 2,000 Native Americans—and as many white people—died in King Philip's War. At least twelve towns were completely destroyed. One of the great tragedies of this war was that the Wampanoag tribe, which had helped the Pilgrims survive their first year, was nearly wiped out.

Another major event in Native American history in the present-day state of Massachusetts was the establishment of "Praying Indian" villages. Beginning in the early 1650s, Reverend John Eliot (known as the "Apostle to the Indians") and other Puritan missionaries attempted to convert Massachusetts, Wampanoags, and other tribes to Christianity. The process demanded that natives permanently live in separate English-type towns, subject to many strict laws

The Wampanoag chief Metacomet—known to the English as King Philip—led an alliance against the English that eventually caused widespread warfare and bloodshed. This engraving depicts the death of Metacomet in 1676, in Kingston, Rhode Island.

regulating hair and dress styles, as well as marriage customs. Eliot translated sermons and the entire Bible into written versions of native languages, which he attempted to teach the "Praying Indians." Between 1651 and 1675, there were as many as fourteen "Praying Indian" villages, perhaps housing up to 1,000 Native Americans, or more. During King Philip's War between 1675 and 1676 some of these Native Americans fought alongside the United Colonies and against members of their own tribes. Most of these "Praying Indians," however, were forced by the English to live on Deer Island in Boston Harbor during the war. Many died on the island as a result of inadequate food and shelter, especially during the bitter winter months.

In Rhode Island

Long before the destruction of King Philip's War, the Englishman Roger Williams often visited Chief Massasoit and learned to speak his language. Williams also traveled to the territory of the Narragansett, in what is now Rhode Island. There he became acquainted with Chief Canonicus and his son Miantonomo. Williams was a well-educated, gentle man who was a minister in the Massachusetts Bay Colony. Unlike many whites, he believed he had much to learn from the native people.

The Narragansett people were peaceful and accepted Williams as a friend. He visited them often and exchanged some of his household goods with them. He gave them mirrors, candles, cloth, and steel needles. They gave him deerskin moccasins and birchbark boxes.

This illustration shows Roger Williams being taken in by the Narragansett after he was banished from the Massachussetts Bay Colony in 1636.

Roger Williams was banished from Massachusetts— forced from the Massachusetts Bay Colony in 1636 and never allowed to return. He had openly disagreed with the severe religious rules of the Puritans, who dominated Massachusetts. He also frequently opposed taking lands from the natives without offering some form of payment.

Williams argued against the beatings and other cruel punishments given to people who did not attend church services or keep the Sabbath. He believed a person should be free to join any church or no church at all. He practiced religious freedom and respect for all religions and peoples.

Williams and his wife needed to choose a place to settle. He appealed to his new friends, the Narragansett, for help. He offered to buy several acres of their land. They welcomed him and gave him many acres at the northern head of Narragansett Bay. He named this area Providence.

Chief Canonicus did not want goods in exchange for land. Instead, he asked Williams to be their peacemaker. In that role, Williams agreed to speak to the English on behalf of the Native Americans when problems arose. The chief knew there would be trouble, as he saw more shiploads of people and guns coming to the area.

In that same year, Roger Williams began applying his peacemaking skills. He discouraged the Narragansett from joining their neighbors, the Pequot, in an attack upon the English in Connecticut. The Pequot were seeking revenge for the murder of one of their men who was accused of killing a colonist. The following year, 1637, the English themselves made a surprise attack on the Pequot and killed some 600 men, women, and children and captured others who were sold into slavery.

More people came from England and joined Williams in the new colony of Rhode Island. To help the newcomers, Williams published a book in 1643, *A Key into the Language of America*. It translated Narragansett phrases into English. It was the first book to record a Native American language.

Williams wrote letters to the leaders of the nearby colonies for the Narragansett when colonists crossed the borders into their land. His efforts as peacemaker were successful for a while. Peaceful times, however, slowly came to an end.

When Roger Williams returned from a long voyage to England, he received sad news. Miantonomo, the son of Chief Canonicus, had been defeated by Chief Uncas of the Mohegans, who delivered him to the English. The English sentenced Miantonomo to death for conspiracy, and he was executed by Uncas's brother. The peaceful Narragansett were gradually drawn into the battles of their neighbors. They opposed King Philip's War in the beginning, but later became active in the conflict. By the end of the war in 1676, most Narragansett had been killed and their villages almost completely destroyed.

A century before Roger Williams met the Narragansett, another European had discovered the fine qualities of these people. Giovanni da Verrazano, an explorer who sailed along the East Coast, visited the tribe in 1524. He wrote in his diary: "These people are the most peaceful and have the most civilized customs we have found on this voyage."

What happened in Virginia, New Netherlands, and New England was similar to what happened in many places along the East Coast. From the late 1600s on, English colonists came in greater numbers to the New World. The number of Native Americans who had lived in the area for thousands of years shrank year by year. Many were killed in battles with Europeans or died from European diseases. Others moved farther west or north to live with other tribes.

In Pennsylvania

Before William Penn set sail for North America in 1682, he sent men ahead of him to make contact with the Native Americans, trade for land, and begin building homes. Penn was determined to start out the right way. He wanted to live together with the natives as peaceful neighbors in the colony he named Pennsylvania. In the end, his plan worked extremely well.

In a letter to several Native American tribes—including the Delaware, Unami, and Lenape—Penn wrote:

My Friends:
 There is one great God and power that hath made the world and all things therein, to whom you and I, and all people owe their being and well-being, and to whom you and I must one day give an account for all that we have done in the world. . .
 I am very sensible of the unkindness and injustice that hath been too much exercised toward you by people of these parts. . . . I have great love and regard to you, and desire to gain your love and friendship by a kind, just and peaceable life. . . .

I am your loving friend,
William Penn

Penn, a Quaker, insisted that the natives be paid fairly for the land that he and others wanted. The land on which Penn's home was built, twenty-five miles upriver from Philadelphia, was traded for 2,000 feet of wampum, plus some Dutch money and many European goods—blankets, kettles, woolen cloth, guns, coats, shirts, stockings, hoes, knives, pipes, combs, scissors, tobacco, rum, cider, and beer. When Penn discovered his secretary had traded liquor, he made a rule that no more alcohol would be traded in the colony.

When Penn arrived in his new colony, he had a meeting with the Delaware under an elm tree at a place called Shackamaxon. That name meant "place of sachems." Sachem is the Native American word for "wise leader" or "chief." Sachems were religious leaders or rulers of allied tribes. Through an interpreter, Penn told his new neighbors the doors of the white people would always be open to them and hoped their doors would also be open as well.

Penn and the chiefs of the Delaware also agreed to form a council to settle differences that might arise. The council

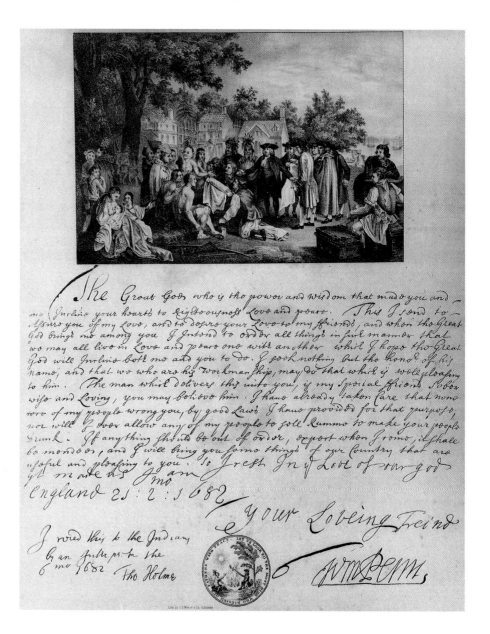

This declaration of love and friendship toward the Native Americans of the Delaware River region was written by William Penn. The engraving that accompanies the letter depicts the first meeting between Penn and the Delaware at a place called Shackamaxon.

of six colonists and six natives would listen to all arguments and decide how to settle problems.

At the end of the meeting, the Delaware were pleased with this remarkable man. They offered him the calumet—the "peace pipe"—as a sign they accepted his plan. They also presented him with a belt of wampum that showed two figures, one with a hat like the Quakers wore.

Years later, a famous French writer, Voltaire, described Penn's relationship with the natives as "the only treaty between Indians and Christians never sworn to and never broken."

Taiment and Tenongham, two sachems of the Unami, became good friends with Penn. He visited their homes and held great feasts for the Native Americans on his property. Penn also became friends with the Susquehanna tribes and treated them as he treated the Delaware.

Penn learned much from his neighbors, particularly about medicine. He was taught how to grind roots and mix them with water to make a healing drink. He also learned how to make a paste, or poultice, from herbs that could be spread over burned skin to heal it and stop infection.

In 1683, Penn wrote a letter to the Free Society of Traders, a group of Quaker friends, about the "Indians" and the new lands. The natives were described as tall and gentle. Their language was made up of words that sounded like music. One or two words of their language, according to Penn, could mean as much as many English words.

Although Penn succeeded in establishing a good relationship with the Native Americans, he had plenty of trouble with the king of England and others in his homeland. He returned to London to settle disputes over taxes and rights to land in Pennsylvania. Before returning to Pennsylvania, he spent almost a year in prison.

Other colonial leaders were having troubles with England and fights with the Native Americans. Penn saw the colonies being drawn into local wars because of what was happening in Europe. Rivalries among rulers of Europe threatened both the colonists and the Native Americans. Penn encouraged colonial leaders to form an alliance of colonies. He died in 1718, nearly fifty years before such an alliance occured.

The Fire-rafts in Detroit River.

Chapter

5

The Effects of the Wars

From 1689 through 1763, the French and English forces fought to control the land between the Appalachian Mountains and the Mississippi River. The French controlled Canada as well as Louisiana. They wanted to connect the two areas by setting up a chain of forts along the rivers. The British also wanted to control that area.

Battles waged between the two European groups always involved the Native Americans. The Mohawk and other Iroquois tribes sided with the British forces. The Ottawa and other northern tribes sided with the French.

Chief Tomochichi, the chief of the Creek people in present-day Georgia, signed a peace treaty with the English. In 1734, General James Oglethorpe, the leader of the English in the Georgia colony, invited Tomochichi and other Creek chiefs to England to meet King George II. They were treated with respect. All the Creek villages signed an alliance with the English and lived in harmony with the settlers until the time of the American Revolution.

Opposite:
Canoes were set ablaze during fighting between Native Americans and the British on the Detroit River in 1763.

49

The French and Indian War

British General Edward Braddock died after being ambushed by French, Canadian, and Indian forces in the French and Indian War.

In 1754, a battle took place for Fort Necessity in western Pennsylvania. This was the first battle of the French and Indian War. The French troops defeated the forces of the Virginia militia led by a young lieutenant colonel named George Washington.

A year later, at Fort Duquesne—on the site of present-day Pittsburgh, Pennsylvania—another battle took place. An Ottawa brave named Pontiac fought on the side of the French, which had a force of 850, including Native Americans. The British colonial forces, Washington among them, had a force of 1,500. The battle was a training ground for two soldiers who would become famous in the years ahead—Washington and Pontiac. The British lost 900 soldiers but left victorious.

For the next nine years, the war between the British and French continued. The British slowly forced the French out of their river forts. In the North, the Ottawa

tribe always had a good relationship with the French. As the French lost power in North America, the Ottawa had to deal with the British, who did not treat them well.

Jeffrey Amherst, the leader of the British forces in 1760, considered all Native Americans savages. He did not trust them and reduced the number of guns and other supplies that the British could trade with them. This act angered the Ottawa and other tribes that were living off the trade. They appealed for help to Pontiac, then an Ottawa chief.

Pontiac believed that an alliance of tribes could defeat the British in the North. The French led Pontiac to believe the French king would support Pontiac if he attacked the British. However, he was misled.

Pontiac was able to organize the Chippewa, Seneca, Potawatomi, Delaware, Shawnee, Winnebago, and Wyandot. This alliance was a major achievement in the history of tribal conflict with white people. Pontiac did what no other Native American had done—unite many tribes for war, even if for only a short period of time.

Rumors of Indian war reached Amherst at his head-quarters in New York. Amherst ignored them. He did not believe that a band of uneducated "savages" could threaten his well-trained forces. He underestimated Pontiac's political and military gifts.

In the course of a year, Native American warriors under Pontiac attacked fourteen British forts from Pennsylvania to Lake Superior. In six weeks they captured ten forts, killing soldiers and taking hostages. They did not succeed in capturing the three largest forts—Niagara, Pitt, and Detroit.

Pontiac himself led the attack on Fort Detroit, which began in May 1763. His forces surrounded the fort and held it under siege from May until October. He arranged his forces in lines around the fort to prevent supplies and reinforcements from reaching the British inside.

Ottawa chief Pontiac holds a council meeting with other Native American leaders. In 1760, Pontiac was able to successfully unite many tribes in a war alliance against the British.

The British trapped in the fort were astounded that the native warriors could sustain such a long and well-planned battle. The soldiers at the fort appealed to Amherst in New York for reinforcements. He at first refused, still thinking the natives too inferior to hold out very long. Finally, he sent more troops. Only then were some of Pontiac's forces turned away. Pontiac finally ended his siege of Fort Detroit in October 1763. He entered into a formal peace agreement at Fort Detroit on August 17, 1765, stating he would never fight again.

The Revolutionary War

During the American Revolution, some Native Americans sided with the British, some sided with the colonists, and many tried to remain out of the conflict. George Washington wrote in 1778:

"I am empowered to employ a body of 400 Indians, if they can be procured on proper terms. . . . I think they may be made excellent use as scouts and light troops, mixed with our own parties."

In the same year, the Delaware people signed a treaty of peace with the new government of the United States. The Native Americans agreed to let the soldiers enter their territories without harm while they attacked the British forts in the area. In return, the Delaware were promised that they could form a state in the new union, but the U.S. government did not keep this promise.

The tribes most affected by the war were the five tribes of the Iroquois. At first, most agreed not to take sides in the conflict, except the Mohawk. Influenced by Joseph Brant, a young Mohawk who had learned to read and write English at a colonial school in Lebanon, Connecticut, the Mohawk took an active part in the war. Brant's sister, Molly, had married the British superintendent of Indian affairs, and Brant himself was made a colonel in the British army. Soon, the other tribes of the Iroquois Confederacy joined him without approval of the Confederacy. The Oneida was the only tribe of the Five Nations Confederacy that did not side with the British. The other tribes all fought alongside the soldiers of General John Burgoyne when he was defeated at Saratoga, New York, in 1777. After that, the war turned in favor of the colonial army led by George Washington.

The final defeat of the British was also a final defeat for the Iroquois nation. They were forced to surrender control of their many lands around the Great Lakes and in what is

General Andrew Jackson was involved in a number of American attacks on Native Americans, including the Creek War of 1813–1814.

now upper New York State. Brant was able to persuade the king of England to give the tribes land in Canada. Today, the land is still called Brant County. It is home to many Mohawk and other tribal descendants.

In the far South, the powerful Creek Confederacy had once sided with the British. When the Creek people saw the English losing the war, they became friendly with the Americans. Alexander McGillivray, a Creek military leader and diplomat, negotiated the Treaty of New York with the Americans in 1790. The Americans made McGillivray a brigadier general in the U.S. Army to ensure the friendly alliance would continue.

McGillivray also held a high position in the Spanish military. The Spanish government still had strong interests in the South and wanted to be on good terms with the powerful Creek Confederacy. McGillivray wanted to protect his people. The Americans never saw McGillivray in his Spanish uniform, and the Spanish never saw this clever Creek soldier in his American uniform.

After Alexander McGillivray's death, the relationship between the members of the Creek Confederacy and Americans turned unfriendly. The Creek people, and all tribes living within or near the new nation, were at a turning point. Their way of life, which had lasted for many centuries, was about to come to an end. The Creek were defeated by the Americans led by General Andrew Jackson in the Creek War of 1813–1814.

Changed Ways

After the American Revolution, Native Americans were removed to reservations and later almost exterminated by the army of the United States.

When the British signed the peace treaty after the war, King George III requested protection for the Native Americans west of the Appalachian Mountains. The Americans agreed to that request, but no one abided by it.

The need for more and more land for the growing nation of Americans led to a policy of removal for native peoples. All remaining tribes of the East were forced to relocate to a place called Indian Territory. It was a dry wasteland, in what is now the state of Oklahoma. Native Americans who had been accustomed to green hills and river valleys were forced to live on reservation lands that could not even grow crops.

Yet the land had one treasure—oil. When oil was discovered in 1904, the Native Americans living in Indian Territory were forced to move again, this time to smaller reservations in the Southwest. Life there for most Native Americans was extremely hard and depressing. They were promised food and help by the U.S. government, but these promises were not kept. Many dishonest government officials filled their own pockets instead of giving the Native Americans needed provisions.

Slowly, from the 1940s forward, Native American life began to improve on the reservations. More and more Native Americans began to live and work with other Americans in towns and cities. Today, Native Americans work in offices and factories, in schools and hospitals, in laboratories and on farms.

This photograph shows an official paying a band of Wisconsin Chippewa in 1871 for land that the tribe agreed to give over to the U.S. government. Later, payments to Native Americans for land were delayed or, more often, simply stopped as previously signed treaties and agreements were ignored by the U.S. government.

INDIAN LAND FOR SALE

GET A HOME

OF

YOUR OWN

✳

EASY PAYMENTS

PERFECT TITLE

✳

POSSESSION

WITHIN

THIRTY DAYS

FINE LANDS IN THE WEST

IRRIGATED
IRRIGABLE
GRAZING
AGRICULTURAL
DRY FARMING

IN 1910 THE DEPARTMENT OF THE INTERIOR SOLD UNDER SEALED BIDS ALLOTTED INDIAN LAND AS FOLLOWS:

Location.	Acres.	Average Price per Acre	Location.	Acres.	Average Price per Acre
Colorado	5,211.21	$7.27	Oklahoma	34,664.00	$19.14
Idaho	17,013.00	24.85	Oregon	1,020.00	15.43
Kansas	1,684.50	33.45	South Dakota	120,445.00	16.53
Montana	11,034.00	9.86	Washington	4,879.00	41.37
Nebraska	5,641.00	36.65	Wisconsin	1,069.00	17.00
North Dakota	22,610.70	9.93	Wyoming	865.00	20.64

FOR THE YEAR 1911 IT IS ESTIMATED THAT 350,000 ACRES WILL BE OFFERED FOR SALE

For information as to the character of the land write for booklet, "INDIAN LANDS FOR SALE," to the Superintendent U. S. Indian School at any one of the following places:

CALIFORNIA: Hoopa. COLORADO: Ignacio. IDAHO: Lapwai. KANSAS: Horton. Nadeau.	MINNESOTA: Onigum. MONTANA: Crow Agency. NEBRASKA: Macy. Santee. Winnebago.	NORTH DAKOTA: Fort Totten. Fort Yates. OKLAHOMA: Anadarko. Cantonment. Colony. Darlington. Muskogee, Pawnee.	OKLAHOMA—Con. Sac and Fox Agency. Shawnee. Wyandotte. OREGON: Klamath Agency. Pendleton. Roseburg. Siletz.	SOUTH DAKOTA: Cheyenne Agency. Crow Creek. Greenwood. Lower Brule. Pine Ridge. Rosebud. Sisseton.	WASHINGTON: Fort Simcoe. Fort Spokane. Tekoa. Tulalip. WISCONSIN: Oneida.

WALTER L. FISHER,
Secretary of the Interior.

ROBERT G. VALENTINE,
Commissioner of Indian Affairs.

Reservations still exist, but they are now controlled by the Native Americans themselves. Some reservation lands are thriving business centers. In the West, the Apache have set up ski resorts on some of their lands. On other lands, they run a prosperous timber business. In the East, the Pequot, who were nearly extinguished by the Pequot Wars in the 1600s, have built the largest Native American casino and entertainment center. The Native Americans and many of their customs have not vanished.

Glossary

ally A person or tribe who joins with another for a common cause, usually defense against enemies.

calumet Sacred object, usually a decorated pipe made of wood and clay-stone, used for peace ceremonies and meetings with important purposes.

confederacy A political union of several tribes that join together for a common purpose.

conquistador Spanish word for "conqueror" or "adventurer."

epidemic The fast spread of a disease throughout a population.

Indian Territory Originally part of the Louisiana Purchase, it was set aside by Congress in 1829 to be used by Native Americans who were forced to move from the East. In 1839, the Cherokee were among the first tribes to be resettled there.

mission A place set up by Christian priests to convert the Indians to Christianity and European customs.

reservation A tract of land that was set aside by the United States for a group of Native Americans. Usually, reservations were small plots of poor-quality land that were offered to Native Americans only after white settlers had seized their lands.

sachem Native American healer thought to be in contact with spirit world. Also refers to a ruler or chief of allied tribes.

wampum Beads made from conch and clam shells, used to make belts that recorded important events in Indian affairs. Wampum was also used as a form of money by European traders in exchange for Indian furs and land.

Further Reading

Bonvillain, Nancy. *Mohawk*. New York: Chelsea House, 1992.

Cwiklid, Robert. *King Philip*. NJ: Silver Burdett Press, 1989.

Doherty, Craig A. and Doherty, Katherine M. *The Huron*. Vero Beach, FL: Rourke, 1994.

_____. *The Narragansett*. Vero Beach, FL: Rourke, 1994.

Grant, Bruce. *Concise Encyclopedia of the American Indian*. Avenal, NJ: Outlet Books, 1989.

Harrington, John P. *Indian Tales from Picuris Pueblo*. Santa Fe, NM: Ancient City Press, 1989.

Hewett, Richard. *Ancient Cliff Dwellers of Mesa Verde*. New York: Clarion Books, 1992.

Katz, William. *Black Indians: A Hidden Heritage*. New York: Macmillan, 1986.

Liptak, Karen. *North American Indian Tribal Chiefs*. New York: Franklin Watts, 1992.

McCall, Barbara A. *The Cherokee*. Vero Beach, FL: Rourke, 1989.

_____. *The Iroquois*. Vero Beach, FL: Rourke, 1989.

Utter, Jack. *American Indians: Answers to Today's Questions*. Lake Ann, MI: National Woodlands Publishing Company, 1993.

Chronology

1540   The Spanish, led by Francisco de Coronado, invade Native American territory in the Southwest.

1565   Spanish soldiers and priests build the mission of St. Augustine, Florida.

1607   Captain John Smith and English colonists establish Jamestown, Virginia.

1608   Samuel de Champlain and French traders invade Huron territory near the St. Lawrence River.

1609   Henry Hudson visits the Mohegan tribe and obtains agreement to build a trading post on what is now the Hudson River in New York.

1621   The Pilgrims and Chief Massasoit of the Wampanoag tribe sign an agreement to live as peaceful neighbors in Massachusetts.

1622   Chief Opechancanough organizes the first coordinated attack on the colonists.

1626   The Dutch "buy" Manhattan Island from Chief Manhassett for goods worth twenty-four dollars.

1636   The Narragansett tribe welcomes Roger Williams into its territory, now Rhode Island.

1675–   Metacomet, a Wampanoag, called King Philip by
1676   the English, wages war against the settlers in New England.

1680   Popé leads the Pueblo Revolt against the Spanish invaders in the Southwest.

1682   The Delaware tribe welcomes William Penn into their territory, now Pennsylvania.

1763   Pontiac, an Ottawa, leads an alliance of tribes in a war against the English forts in the Northeast.

Index

970.01 3 2751 90001 2667
MCC
c.1
$16.95

McCall, Barbara

AUTHOR
The European Invasion

TITLE

DATE DUE	BORROWER'S NAME	ROOM NUMBER
10/11	Wilmarie lopez	~~108~~
4/23	Gladisy Sancha	120
2/22	Giovani S.	107
10 20	Eddie	
1/25		

3 2751 90001 2667
c.1
$16.95

970.01
MCC

McCall, Barbara
The European Invasion

10/11	
4/3	
2/22	
10/20	
1/25	
3/3	